IMPERFECTION

EXPLORING EMOTIONS, EMBRACING IMPERFECTIONS

AASHNA MADAN

Made with ♥ on the Notion Press Platform
www.notionpress.com

The Kindness Foundation is a non-profit and kindness movement that is dedicated to promoting kindness, empathy, and compassion as the pillars of a better world. We run several programs, workshops and events year-round to not only inspire kindness in daily life but also create positive change.

The International Kindness Festival (IKF) is the first of its' kind global celebration of kindness. It is a platform where we share ideas, stories, and experiences that illuminate the path toward a world steeped in kindness.

We strongly believe that it is our youth who are poised to create positive change. The **Book Release event**, a part of the **International Kindness Festival 2023**, is a unique opportunity for our youth to share a piece of their soul through the written word and/or artistic expression, and get their work published. Recognising that being comfortable with your authenticity is a superpower and a form of kindness to self.

ACKNOWLEDGEMENTS

Maya Thiagarajan – Founder, TREE Learning
Diana Shathish – Art Educator & Entrepreneur
Notion Press Publishing

Contents

1. Perfection 1

2. A Way Of Life 3

3. Home Sweet Home 4

4. Petrichor 5

5. Leaving 6

6. Ostracised 7

7. Fake It Till You Make It 8

8. Bedbugs 9

9. Fever 10

10. A Good Day 12

11. The Crushing Wait 13

12. Togetherness 14

13. A Tough Time 15

14. Gratitude 16

1. Perfection

A thorn in her heart,
A needle pricking her soul,
She walks straight, perfectly,
Perfectly, hiding her imperfection.
Her whole life is a play,
She is layered by a costume,
All the words that come out of her lips,
All dialogues are part of a perfect script.
Her beauty is an illusion,
Her smile has engraved hidden pain,
Her face smothered with blush,
To bring some colour to her face,
To hide the darkness in her face.
Her happiness is sadness,
Her heart weak with grief,
Her mind clogged with trying to be perfect,
Each breath with false perfection.
Hypnotised into a hoax,
Sucked into an alternate reality,
Engulfed into an unhealthy world,
Where ceaseless perfection is effortless and untiring.
Her weakness for perfection,
Causes her unreal craving,
Breaking down her soul,
Cracking her shattered heart.
Perfection damaging her,

Blocking the light,
Hiding the happiness,
Making her imperfections the spotlight.
A mirror opposite her,
Reflects her imperfections,
Her craving for perfection,
Breaks and shatters her,
Like a cracked mirror,
Not able to be put together again.

2. A way of Life

Ink spread over hands,
Head pounding, fingers aching,
Papers flailed on the floor
Tear droplets emerge.
Falling swiftly into an orb of anxiety, Laptop
glaring, as the screen becomes blurry, Eyes
squinting, brain dead,
Ideas combust at every attempt to think.
Sleep as an escape
A fire exit in the middle of raging panic
Except a loophole, the awakening,
The reconstruction of the mind.
Heaven to hell,
A sanctuary to a dungeon,
Locked out, the key missing
The key to success.
Recovery is tough,
Rehabilitation is often gradual
As the world becomes one,
The next wildfire brews.

3. Home sweet Home

When your demons possess you,
When your brain doesn't work,
When you're alone and broken,
Home is a glue that holds you together; unbreakable.
Sometimes more often than not,
Home feels different from a sanctuary,
Because of internal anger and pain,
A bubbling flask, a recipe for disaster.
Even with your changes and moods,
Your home will always stay with you.
You might not value what a home means,
But when you need it, a true home will always be there for you.
Often, when you are lost and cannot be found
When you trip and fall down, struggling to get up
Home is a guaranteed place of rest,
A place to pause for a second in a time-bound world.
A home doesn't have to be a roof over heads,
It doesn't have to be a specific location,
Home is not just a word, it's an emotion
It can be a person, it can be a place.

4. Petrichor

Pitter, patter on the window
Drizzles of rainfall,
The putrid scent of wet grass and mud,
From droplets slowly changes to
floods.
Menacingly, clouds roaring,
Yelling out curses and taunts
Representing the pain in humans,
Bringing out their inner demons.
Suffocating us inside this bubble of water,
Sinking deeper and deeper, unable to breathe
Monsters hiding with us underneath our beds
Ghosts of the sky haunting from the dead.
Beating like a drum, thunderous shouts,
Flashes of lights causing tremors within,
Knee-deep in panic, knee-deep in fear, Not
quite aware of the troubles that are near.
Nowhere to run, nowhere to hide,
Each and every crevice blocked,
An obstacle course, not ready for the ride,
Eyes alert, yet the heart doesn't abide.
As the world is silenced, worry begins to dissipate,
Calmness fills the air, petrichor awakens individuals and
families.
Until the next day, when another pitter-patter calls
out, The nightmare returns, with screams and shouts.

5. Leaving

A far away, unknown place,
One which is supposed to feel like home,
Sailing away from what feels like yours,
Not sure how to go back, not sure how to move forward.
The journey is terrifying, yet has a thrill,
New paths to explore, new chapters to unfold,
New memories ready to be developed,
A new life is waiting to start.
But what about the old?
Old friends, old school, old shelter,
Old paths, old chapters, old memories,
Will I be able to easily let them go?
A little sister growing up,
Some hairs turning grey,
Seeing my family's loving faces at dawn,
And saying goodnight at dusk.
Goodnight to my home,
Goodnight to my friends and family,
Goodnight to my memories,
Yet, a goodnight isn't a goodbye.
There will always be dreams,
Chats at strange hours,
A lasting bond, always,
No matter how far my journey takes me.

6. Ostracised

An unpleasant air of distress,
Sitting quietly on the hallway steps,
There was a time when there was no one,
No one to call a friend.
Eating lunch in a corner alone,
The bland cafeteria food increasing my distaste,
Yet, no one to share my sorrows with,
No one who understands my plight.
In the classroom, yelling out proud,
Even the teachers wished I didn't make a sound,
However bubbly, however loud,
I wasn't accepted into the crowd.
Forced to withdraw my personality from the race,
Forced to change every aspect of my being,
Forced to run and forced to hide,
Forced to create a new definition of myself.
Soon I quietened, soon I settled,
Soon I managed to fit in,
Traces of the old me still remained,
Even though it was bleak, an almost invisible trail.
I found people who accepted me for me,
Even though I had to make a few tweaks,
People who loved me, embraced me as a whole,
People who prevent me from, again, falling down a hole.

7. Fake It Till You Make It

A smile plastered on my face,
A frown pinched upside down,
Tear glands strangled,
Eyes painted back to brown.
The sky drenched with cold water and air,
Falling upon the earth, the wind in my hair,
Looking into the sky, praying for a rain holiday
A glimmer of hope goes a long way.
Trying to wake up with enthusiasm,
Yet, in my reflection, I see a frown,
It takes energy just to get up,
For that small task, I feel the need for a crown.

Look lively, be calm,
Smile through the sadness,
Smile through the stress,
Smile, smile, smile,
Be happy.

8. Bedbugs

I am not an insomniac,
Yet lately I sleep very late,
As my head hits the pillow I fall asleep,
Taking this for granted.
People can't choose their fate,
People can't decide what they will get,
Rest or no rest is not up to a few,
Despite this, we are awake at one or two.
For some, sleep is an escape,
Taking naps as soon as life gets tough,
But that isn't the most foolproof way,
As when you wake up, you are greeted by the same day.
Same worries, clearer head?
Is the answer a blanket and a bed?
Or is it more intense?
A different approach, a different lens.
Life can often be overwhelming,
We have nowhere else to go,
No other choice but to take a break, preventing wear and tear,
Just hoping that there is a dream instead of nightmares.

9. Fever

Dread erupting in the middle of the night,
3 AM head pounding, temperatures rising
Even though the air conditioning is at its lowest degree,
Burning, as I limp to other rooms.
Sweat dripping from my pale skin,
My body trying to not dissolve
Into a pool of nothing,
Burning, as I try to find the light.
Thoughts scrambling in my head,
Trying to articulate and form words
Like it was a game of scrabble,
Burning, attempting to make my next move.
The maze of life was coming closer,
I don't know how to get to the end,
Each step a chore, each rush, limbs feeling like they tore
Burning, caution, the effort it took not to fall.
Feeling like a bird, amidst a glass room,
Dizzy, spinning, waves of panic,
Searching for hope amidst the chaos,
Burning, trying not to surrender to the blinding lights.
Praying to find another soul around,
Craving a crutch, something to hold on to
Waiting for my power and strength to reincarnate
Burning, frying in a pan of anxiety.
Knees giving in, sinking to the ground,
Gripping on to the last inches of might,

Burning, burning, burning,
Burning, burning; too bright.

10. A Good Day

Waking up to a chirpy morning,
The atmosphere is breezy, and rays of sun interrupt me,
There's a little nip in the air,
Something wonderful is going to happen today.
Breakfast with the family, a grand opening to the day,
The barking of dogs does not upset me,
The long scroll of assignments doesn't worry me
Small discrepancies cannot faze the joy I see.
Slurping my favourite ice cream, a brain freeze does not ache,
Sweet and cold, a visit to a dentist I do not anticipate
My grandmother's jelly and custard served on a silver platter,
Devouring the goodness, my smile did not falter.
The sky was clear, the pleasant weather giving me a shiver,
The divine clouds were peaceful, there was no thunder to be heard,
A powerful sensation drifted through my bones,
Yet, another day when the rain did not disturb.
My home was a sanctuary, protecting me from the demons outside,
I don't feel my usual exhaustion, relaxation is a constant state,
It almost makes me forget
About the pandemic outside, that we all hate.

11. The Crushing Wait

How I long for one of those fairy tales
Where one doesn't have to bother
About anything in the world,
It's just meant to be.
Being alone is not something one should fear, but
when I think about forever it's not so clear, I really
want something real, I know the time will come, but
I can't help but think how it happens for some.
I love the idea of something old-fashioned,
I love the idea of waiting for the right moment,
But the right moment never seems to reach,
Waiting, waiting, just waiting.
Flowers. Music. Dance.
The true deal, the fantasy,
Does one have to base it all on chance,
Or is there a way to make the stars align?
Stars. Sunset. Light.
The genuine feelings, the bliss,
The passion with all its might,
However slow, however sudden.
I might not have experienced it, but I'm
sure if I wait, soon I will, to see what the
future has in store for us, looking out the
window sill.

12. Togetherness

There are moments in life that make me feel grateful,
When everyone is together in one place
Laughing and joking when sitting in a circle,
Sharing old memories and reminiscing.
Sometimes I love the excuses to have a gathering,
In town for work, a random function, a wedding,
However short a while, I cannot ever forget them,
These experiences are a snapshot in my mind and heart.
I recall the guests that entered my home,
Old friends of my family,
I'd get a glimpse of their days,
Get reminded that there were other times.
Hearing childhood stories from people
Is always a little strange
As their lives were so different
And mine was not on the same page.
So many truths uncover,
So many hidden pieces of knowledge I learn,
When I just take the time
To spend time with others around.
It's like looking into a camera roll,
Taking a peek out of my own life
And into the lives of others,
For once learning to listen instead of speak.

13. A Tough Time

My first loss in life, my first real one,
Back when I thought sadness was when I couldn't submit my homework on time,
I thought loss was when I had a cold and couldn't attend my friend's birthday party,
I was so wrong.
A loss of a loved one sometimes doesn't hit you immediately,
But sometimes it does, and it felt like there was no getting back from it,
Seeing your family cry isn't something I would wish upon my worst enemy,
I didn't know how to be strong, how to be back to my energetic self.
It wasn't completely unexpected and sudden,
I always assumed it would happen one day,
One day in the far future,
Even if it was anticipated, it didn't make it less painful.
I know better now, I know there is a way to forget about the sorrow,
A way to think of the fond memories and smile,
But to see everyone so vulnerable at every anniversary,
Brings a small part of it back, the horror felt when first finding out.
The guilt that you feel, once it soon fades into a memory,
You want to remember your moments with them, but it's just a blur in the past,
You feel the emotions but cannot put a direct face to it,
You know it's wrong, but you don't know how to fix it.
At the end of the day, life goes on,
We need to be able to cope,
It may take some time and a few bad days, but recovery
is not impossible, however much it may feel like it.

14. Gratitude

I feel like I don't appreciate my life enough,
When there is so much joy in it,
I complain when it isn't that tough,
I sometimes just need to be grateful, a bit.
I'm thankful for my loving family,
They are my pillars when I am down,
They truly support me and take care of me gladly,
They make me feel like I've been enthroned a crown.
I'm thankful for my growing friendships,
The real ones who have stuck by me,
Through all my mood swings, rants and trips,
Around them, myself, I can truly be.
I don't appreciate my privilege enough,
A good home, food on my plate every day,
Some people's life, it's rough,
Basic necessities are easy access per se.
I live in a safe environment, not only
Physically, I've always felt safe to share my
thoughts, no fear of judgement, all relief, less
anxiety, being my creative self, not bound by knots.
I watch documentaries on refugees and their lives,
They make me feel free and independent, thriving,
When my biggest concerns are when my exams arrive,
And theirs are trying to keep surviving.
I'm thankful I'm young and I have time to figure life out,
I'm scared to claim responsibility and peek into adulthood,

Often fear evades me along with confusion and doubt,
Yet the future is far away, I still have time, I'll be fine and good.

www.ingramcontent.com/pod-product-compliance
Lightning Source LLC
LaVergne TN
LVHW040942150826
845672LV00008B/2496

* 9 7 9 8 8 9 1 8 6 4 8 0 1 *